GOD'S HEALING *Touch*

IT'S HIS WILL. IT'S FOR TODAY. IT'S FOR YOU!

BY RICHARD ROBERTS

Unless otherwise noted, scripture quotations are taken from the New King James Version® Copyright © 1982 by Thomas Nelson. Used by permission. All rights reserved.

Scripture quotations marked AMP are from the Amplified Version, copyright © 1954, 1958, 1962, 1964, 1965, 1987, 2015 by Zondervan and The Lockman Foundation. Used by permission.

Scripture quotations marked MSG are taken from THE MESSAGE, copyright © 1993, 2002, 2018 by Eugene H. Peterson. Used by permission of NavPress, represented by Tyndale House Publishers. All rights reserved.

Scripture quotations marked KJV are from the King James Version of the Bible.

Copyright © 2022
By Richard Roberts
Tulsa, Oklahoma

ISBN 978-1-7346612-4-8

Published by Oral Roberts Evangelistic Association,
DBA Richard Roberts Ministries
PO Box 2187 • Tulsa, OK 74102-2187

All rights reserved.

Printed in the United States of America

INTRODUCTION

Throughout all of my life, I have known the healing power of God. Being the son of Oral Roberts, a world-renowned evangelist in the healing ministry, set me in an atmosphere for miracles. Even as a boy, I traveled with my father watching and learning as he preached and prayed for the sick.

Now, someone may ask the question, *Was everyone he prayed for healed?* No… But a lot were.

There were many times in my childhood when my dad prayed for me. And most of the time when he did, I received a healing.

I remember once when I had 22 warts on my left hand. My dad prayed for me and all the warts disappeared.

When I was 19, my dad prophesied over me saying that God had called me to a healing ministry. At the time, I didn't fully understand. All I knew was, I hated sickness and God was a Healer. I knew Exodus 15:26 which says, *"I am the Lord that health thee."*

Also, because of the teachings and actions of the apostle Paul in the Bible, I knew that God heals through many different methods. He heals through the laying on of hands. He heals as people release their faith for a miracle. He heals by sending His Word... *He sent his word, and healed them, and delivered them from their destructions* (Psalm 107:20).

He heals through our standing upon and confessing healing scriptures. He heals through the operation of the gifts of the Holy Spirit. He heals by using Bible-honored points of contact, like prayer cloths and anointing oil. He heals by people praying for one another, according to James 5:16.

God is sovereign and can heal us any way He chooses.

I have written this book to give some details about how the healing ministry flows through the lives of believers and to show you beyond any doubt that it is God's will for you to be healed...in every area of your life.

Richard Roberts

Table of Contents

Chapter 1
What I Believe About Healing 7

Chapter 2
Today, Let's Settle the Issue 11

Chapter 3
Seven Reasons Why Jesus Heals and Still Heals Today 15

Chapter 4
Faith that Moves Your Mountain 23

Chapter 5
God Is on Your Side. 27

Chapter 6
Wilt Thou Be Made Whole? 31

Chapter 7
Seven Rules of Faith to Change Your Life 35

Chapter 8
A Holy Determination 45

Chapter 9
A Miracle Settles the Issue 51

Chapter 10
I Hate Cancer! 55

Chapter 11
You Are a Part of Your Answer 61

Chapter 12
Fueled by Faith 67

Chapter 13
Summary 71

CHAPTER 1

What I Believe about Healing

All healing comes from God. This statement is the beginning and the ending for the premise of this book. No "ifs, ands or buts."

I believe, and most Christians will tell you they believe, all healing comes from God. However, I never cease to be amazed when someone raises the question of whether God still heals people today.

And, I also believe—and will give you biblical proof for it in this writing—that healing is God's will, it's for today and I believe it's for you!

God said in Malachi 3:6, *For I am the Lord, I change not.* And the Bible tells us in Hebrews 13:8 that *Jesus Christ—God's only Son, who was the representation of the Father in the earth—is the same yesterday, today and forever.* So, the answer to the question of whether or not He still heals today is an emphatic Yes!

In my life and ministry, I've seen many, many healing miracles. I've ministered in more than thirty countries around the world and have witnessed healings in every one of those countries.

God can and does heal in a variety of ways… He uses prayer aligned with our faith, He uses doctors and medicines and He will use climate, diet, exercise and thinking good thoughts. He sometimes uses a "point of contact" such as prayer cloths or anointing oil. The apostle Paul used a point of contact in his ministry when he placed cloths upon people who were ill or demon-possessed…cloths which had touched his own body… and special miracles occurred.

But whether it is physical healing, emotional healing, financial healing, or healing in a relationship, God wants you to know that it is His will to heal you. He's still in the miracle-working business and He has not taken down His "Open for Business" sign.

In Matthew 6:10, Jesus taught His disciples—and us—how to pray. It's known commonly as "The Lord's Prayer." In it, He teaches us to pray for His will to be done on earth, as it is in Heaven.

Well, what are things like in Heaven? It's a place where there is no pain, no sin, no loneliness, poverty or sickness. So, we can conclude that it is indeed God's will to set His people free from such things here on earth.

Jesus knew His Father's will and that He had been given the authority to forgive sin and to heal. And that's exactly how Jesus lived His life during His earthly ministry, demonstrating Heaven and representing the Father. Through Jesus' death on the Cross and through His resurrection, He purchased both your forgiveness and your healing. *But he was wounded for our transgressions, he was bruised for our iniquities: the chastisement of our peace was upon him; and with his stripes we are healed* (Isaiah 53:5).

Jesus is—today—a Healing Jesus. And I believe He wants to heal *you!*

MY HEALING CONFESSIONS...

- *Because Jesus provided abundant life for me—I can live a life of health, prosperity and freedom in Him.* (John 10:10)
- *I will believe for and receive every good and perfect gift that comes down from the Father.* (James 1:17)

CHAPTER 2

Today, Let's Settle the Issue

Beloved, I pray that you may prosper in all things and be in health, just as your soul prospers. —3 John 2

Matthew 9:35 tells us… *Jesus went about all the cities and villages, teaching in their synagogues, preaching the gospel of the kingdom and healing every sickness and every disease among the people.*

Notice that Matthew did not say Jesus healed only people with certain qualifications or certain diseases or conditions, or that He healed only some of the illnesses which people brought to Him for healing.

No! It says that Jesus healed *every* sickness and *every* disease among the people.

Luke, who was Jesus' disciple and a physician, related in Acts 10:38… *How God anointed Jesus of Nazareth with the Holy Ghost and with power: who went about doing good, and healing all that were oppressed of the devil; for God was with him.*

Jesus never turned away anyone who came to Him for healing… and He will not turn you away today.

Jesus has compassion toward you (Matthew 14:14). He knows right where you are, where you've been and what you are going through.

If you need healing or someone you know needs healing or you've been through some other kind of tragedy and you are asking if this situation, this sickness or disease, this financial mess you're in is some kind of punishment from God, let me assure you that it is not. In fact, I don't believe anything could be further from the truth.

We have to get it straight in our minds and in our spirits from the get-go that God does not put sickness and disease or any bad thing upon us.

However, there is an enemy in the world—an enemy of God and an enemy of ours because we believe and follow after God. His name is Satan, the devil, the *accuser of the brethren* (Revelation 12:10).

Jesus also called the devil a thief and said in John 10:10… *"The thief does not come except to steal, and to kill, and to destroy. I have come that they may have life, and that they may have it more abundantly."*

First John 3:8 tells us… *He who sins is of the devil, for the devil has sinned from the beginning.* **For this purpose** *the Son of God was manifested,* **that He might destroy the works of the devil***.*

So, if you should begin to question whether or not a sickness or some other unfortunate circumstance is from God, ask yourself… Is what I'm experiencing part of the abundant life Jesus came to give me, or is it something which can destroy my life? If it isn't adding to your quality of life and making it better, then it isn't from God. It's from the devil.

Jesus gives abundantly and over-and-above anything we can either think or ask (Ephesians 3:20). Satan wants to steal from us, kill us and/or destroy everything good in our lives.

Know this… **God is a good God and the devil is a bad devil.** It makes no sense for a good God to put something bad on you.

God is for you and the devil is against you. The attack that has come against you is not from God. It's from the devil.

Today, right now, determine to put the blame where the blame belongs and settle this issue…once and for all. Begin to believe that God wants you well, and be expecting His miracles.

MY HEALING CONFESSIONS…

- *God has a good plan for my life; a plan that's for my benefit and not for my harm.* (Jeremiah 29:11)
- *I believe God wants me well and I roll any doubts over onto Him.* (Mark 9:24)

CHAPTER 3

Seven Reasons Why Jesus Heals and Still Heals Today

I don't know why some people, even those who are believers, think that miracles don't happen today or that they ended in Bible days. Maybe it's because we're not seeing miracles on such a broad scale as were seen during Jesus' earthly ministry. But in my heart, I believe it has more to do with a lack of faith rather than a reluctance on Jesus' part to perform miracles in our lives.

There are those who teach that there were three specific hundred-year periods of time in history when God performed miracles. First, in the days of Moses and Joshua. Second, in the days of Elijah and Elisha and third, when Jesus and His disciples walked the earth.

But, why would Jesus heal people back in Bible days and then leave the rest of us throughout history to fend for ourselves? You are loved just as much as He loved the woman with the issue of blood whom He healed. (See the gospels of Matthew, Mark and

Luke.) He is as quick to forgive you when you repent of sin as He was to forgive the thief on the cross beside Him.

The truth is, Jesus did not leave us alone to bear sickness and illness, nor to drag through life under a burden of sin.

Jesus told His disciples right before His time on earth was over... *And I will pray the Father, and He will give you another Helper, that He may abide with you forever—the Spirit of truth, whom the world cannot receive, because it neither sees Him nor knows Him; but you know Him, for He dwells with you and will be in you. I will not leave you orphans; I will come to you* (John 14:16-18).

As Jesus was the representation of God on earth, the Holy Spirit is the representation of Jesus, in us. If we have asked Jesus to be the Lord and Savior of our life, He, the Holy Spirit, comes to dwell with us and is in us. And that's how Jesus still performs miracles today, through the work of the Holy Spirit and by our faith. *Does the God who lavishly provides you with his own presence, his Holy Spirit, working things in your lives you could never do for yourselves, does he do these things because of your strenuous moral striving or because you trust him to do them in you? Don't these things happen among you just as they happened with Abraham? He believed God, and that act of belief was turned into a life that was right with God* (Galatians 3:5-6 MSG).

Now that we've established that Jesus does still heal today, let me give you *7 Reasons Why Jesus Still Heals Today*...

Jesus heals because of His compassion. Jesus became "as one of us" while He was on the earth. He felt the same feelings, hurts and emotions that we feel. So, when He felt compassion, He was moved to help, to bring about change. And, miracles confirmed that He was who He said He was. *For we do not have a High Priest who cannot sympathize with our weaknesses, but was in all points tempted as we are, yet without sin. Let us* *therefore come boldly to the throne of grace, that we may obtain mercy and fnd grace to help in time of need* (Hebrews 4:15-16).

Jesus heals to show us healing belongs to us. In Matthew 15, we learn that Jesus was approached by a Canaanite woman (not of the Jewish faith) and asked Him for healing for her daughter who was demon possessed... *And behold, a woman of Canaan came from that region and cried out to Him, saying, "Have mercy on me, O Lord, Son of David! My daughter is severely demon-possessed." But He answered her not a word. And His disciples came and urged Him, saying, "Send her away, for she cries out after us." But He answered and said, "I was not sent except to the lost sheep of the house of Israel." Then she came and worshiped Him, saying, "Lord, help me!" But He answered and said, "It is not good to take the children's bread and throw it to the little dogs." And she said, "Yes, Lord, yet even the little dogs eat the crumbs which fall from their masters' table." Then Jesus answered and said to her, "O woman, great is your faith! Let it be to you as you desire." And her daughter was healed from that very hour.*

Jesus heals to fulfill the prophecy of healing. In 1 Peter 2:24, we learn, *"...and by his stripes we WERE healed."* Healing is part of what Jesus came to secure for you through His death on the Cross and resurrection.

Jesus heals to reveal His Father's glory. *Then great multitudes came to Him, having with them the lame, blind, mute, maimed, and many others; and they laid them down at Jesus' feet, and He healed them. So the multitude marveled when they saw the mute speaking, the maimed made whole, the lame walking, and the blind seeing; and they glorifed the God of Israel* (Matthew 15:30-31). Miracles draw a crowd. Whenever God does a miracle, it reveals His power, glory and goodness.

Jesus heals to prove His mission. *He who has seen Me has seen the Father...* (John 14:9). Jesus came to show us God's love in action and to bring us salvation, healing and deliverance in every area of life.

Jesus heals to destroy the works of the devil. *For this purpose the Son of God was manifested, that He might destroy the works of the devil* (1 John 3:8). Sickness and every evil thing are works of the enemy. Jesus came to destroy that work. *And the Lord will deliver me from every evil work and preserve me for His heavenly kingdom* (2 Timothy 4:18).

Jesus heals to prove He is the Messiah. God's miracles reinforce the message of the gospel.

I have conducted healing services and crusades around the world and have witnessed thousands of healing miracles. I want to share three with you that stand out in my mind because they each represent and confirm some or all of the seven points I made above…

One night during a crusade in Jos, Nigeria, I noticed a sudden stirring in the crowd. Then I saw this young man come walking up and stand upon the platform, and he began to go back and forth across the platform. The people in the crowd were screaming and cheering. I didn't know what the deal was! I knew there must have been some miracle, but I didn't know what the story was until later. Apparently he was brought to my meeting.

Abdul was a young Muslim man, about 22 years of age. He was a beggar who sat every day in front of the post office in Jos, Ni-geria. He was very popular in the city and known by everyone. Abdul had never walked. He had never stood. He could only crawl on his hands and knees.

But during my meeting, as I prayed, he began to feel the power of God surging through him and he was able to stand and to walk for the first time in his life.

Abdul was later interviewed by the press and they carried his testimony on the front page of the newspaper. It was unprecedented and was better advertisement for our crusade than we could have ever put out! In one city the radio station, which was owned by the government, made an announcement that Richard Roberts was holding a miracle healing crusade… *Come and bring your sick so they can be healed.*

This next miracle healing was just recently confirmed again in one of my recent healing services…

Nine-year-old Emily Dia lived in Alabama and she loved horses. However, she had a hard time riding horses because she had been born with bowed legs, which caused both of her feet to turn inward. Doctors told her parents that her legs might straighten as she got older and her left leg did, but not her right leg. It still turned inward. Her turned-in foot inside the stirrup on the saddle of a horse made it nearly impossible for Emily to get the horse to do what she wanted.

Her turned-in foot also caused her to trip a lot, even over the smallest gravel. She would actually trip over her own crooked foot because as she walked, it would throw itself in front of the other foot. It made it especially hard as she tried to keep up with her two younger brothers.

Doctors gave Emily's parents the option of surgery but instead, they felt God leading them to begin watching more Christian TV programming as they prayed and sought a healing for little Emily.

As a family, they soon began watching Lindsay and me on our TV program and right before Easter one year, when Emily was nine, I encouraged people at home watching our show to take communion with us. The atmosphere was ripe for God's miracles and we were all in expectation.

Emily told her mom she wanted to take communion.

She and her family gathered up the ingredients, the bread and the juice, and they all participated with us.

Five minutes before the show was to end, I had a word of knowledge that God was healing someone who had a crooked foot. I said, "If any of you have a crooked foot, touch it and believe for it to turn straight."

(If you are unfamiliar with the term "word of knowledge," it's one of the nine gifts of the Spirit and is supernatural information from God that comes into the heart or mind of a believer. Further information on the workings of the Holy Spirit can be found on our website at RichardRoberts.org.)

So little Emily reached down and touched her foot. She said it was warm, sort of tingly but felt good. And then… as she watched, it turned straight! Emily jumped up, shouting and screaming and hugging her mama and yelling that her foot was straight. She ran down the hallway and jumped up and down. She said, "It felt so strong and it was so straight!" Her mom related that her calf was also straight and just like the other one.

Emily could now run and play with her brothers without tripping…and ride her horses better.

Now, for the rest of the story… Today, Emily is a grown woman in her twenties and recently attended one of my services in Alabama. She gave her testimony again and showed everyone that she is still healed by the power of God. Her foot is still straight and she can do anything that others do. She is currently getting her Master's Degree in accounting. Praise the Lord!

The third miracle healing is about Jennifer, a dentist who helped out in one of our medical clinics and crusades in Guatemala City, received a healing of her own.

"Twenty years ago, Richard Roberts came to Guatemala in a crusade for miracles. At the time, I was in the hospital with leukemia. I was not expected to survive.

"My grandmother was a believer and she had heard that Richard was coming to Guatemala City, so she took me out of the hospital, believing I would be healed that night. The doctor told her, 'If you take your granddaughter out of the hospital, she may die.' But, my grandmother had faith in Jesus' power to heal.

"At the crusade, Richard prayed for me. I had a vision and saw a bright light, which then changed into the figure of a man. He wore a mantle, which was bright like the light I had seen. In my spirit I knew that I only had to touch Him and I was going to be healed.

"The Man in my vision laid His hand on my head and said, 'Don't be afraid. You are healed.' It was the most incredible moment in my life! I went to the floor and my grandmother thought I had died but Jesus was healing me. I soon stood up and said, 'I am healed.'

"The next day, I had an exam with my doctor. He looked at the test results and said, 'I don't know what happened, but everything is well.' My healing was confirmed!"

It should also be noted that ten of the other children in the hospital with her when she was ill died. She was the only survivor.

My friend, you'll never convince me that God does not heal. Nothing is too hard for Him! Miracles are still for today—and miracles are for YOU!

MY HEALING CONFESSIONS...

- *I am God's property! The devil has no authority in my life to try to steal, kill and destroy.* (John 10:10)

- *I believe Jesus is the same yesterday, today and forever and that His healing is for me today—in the now of my life—just as in Bible days.* (Hebrews 13:8)

CHAPTER 4

Faith that Moves Your Mountain

Jesus said to them, "… for assuredly, I say to you, if you have faith as a mustard seed, you will say to this mountain, 'Move from here to there,' and it will move; and nothing will be impossible for you. —Matthew 17:20

Why don't more Christians have mountain-moving faith? Is it that we don't really believe that moving a mountain [a problem] out of the way with our faith is actually possible? Or maybe we think we don't have enough faith or the right kind of faith.

Well, let's first address this last statement. The Bible says in Romans 12:3 that God gave each person the measure of faith. Now, a lot of Bible translations might say "a" measure of faith. But I like the King James Version which says "the" measure of faith. That means that God gave each one of us just enough faith and we all have the same amount.

And we can see from the verse at the beginning of this chapter that we only need faith the size of a mustard seed. Now, the mustard seed is one of the tiniest seeds in the world. Yet, when it is planted, it can produce a tree big enough for the birds of the air to rest on its branches. (See Matthew 13:32)

God gives each of us THE measure of faith to start out with. And as we grow and mature in the knowledge of Him and His ways of doing and being, our faith matures also.

In Mark chapter 9, Jesus had just come off a tremendous experience with Peter, James and John on the Mount of Transfiguration. They came down the mountain only to find the other nine disciples and a distraught man and his son...

And when He came to the disciples, He saw a great multitude around them, and scribes disputing with them. Immediately, when they saw Him, all the people were greatly amazed, and running to Him, greeted Him. And He asked the scribes, "What are you discussing with them?" Then one in the crowd answered and said, "Teacher, I brought You my son, who has a mute spirit. And wherever it seizes him, it throws him down; he foams at the mouth, gnashes his teeth, and becomes rigid. So, I spoke to Your disciples, that they should cast it out, but they could not." He answered him and said, "O faithless generation, how long shall I be with you? How long shall I bear with you? Bring him to Me." Then they brought him to Him. And when he saw Him, immediately the spirit convulsed him, and he fell on the ground and wallowed, foaming at the mouth. So He asked his father, "How long has this been happening to him?" And he said, "From childhood. And often he has thrown him both into the fire and into the water to destroy him. But if You can do anything, have compassion on us and help us." Jesus said to him, "If you can believe, all things are possible to him who believes." Immediately the father of the child cried out and said with tears, "Lord, I believe; help my unbelief!" When Jesus saw that the people came running together, He rebuked the unclean spirit, saying to it, "Deaf and dumb spirit, I command you, come out of him and enter him no more!" Then the spirit cried out, convulsed him greatly, and came out of him. And he became as one dead, so that many said, *"He is dead."* But Jesus took him by the hand and lifted him up, and he arose (Mark 9:14-27 KJV).

Jesus said, *"O, faithless generation…"* Is that what we've become? Are we a faithless generation? Can we only believe for small things, mere mole hills, and not for extravagant miracles from a loving God? Or can we truly believe to move mountains?

Is that how you feel concerning this sickness, this disease, this financial problem, this family problem, this job-related problem you're experiencing…trying to believe but needing help with your unbelief?

Jesus said in the story above, "Bring him to me." And that's the solution to moving your mountain…take it to Jesus. *Trust in the Lord with all your heart, and lean not on your own understanding; In all your ways acknowledge Him, and He shall direct your paths* (Proverbs 3:5-6).

Maybe you would reply as the father of the boy did… "Yes, Lord, I do believe, but help my unbelief." In other words, "Yes, Lord, I do believe, but I have this little pocket of doubt and it plagues me all the time. You see, Jesus, this problem—this sickness, financial distress, past mistakes—have been with me for so long and I've been carrying all this fear, worry, guilt and depression. It seems like it just won't let me go. I've prayed, I've studied the Bible and I've stood in faith. I've done everything I know to do but it's still here."

I tell you, God's Word has the remedy…

Come to Me, all you who labor and are heavy laden, and I will give you rest. Take My yoke upon you and learn from Me, for I am gentle and lowly in heart, and you will find rest for your souls. For My yoke is easy and My burden is light" (Matthew 11:28-30).

…take up the whole armor of God, that you may be able to withstand

in the evil day, and having done all, to stand (Ephesians 6:13).

And let us not grow weary while doing good, for in due season we shall reap if we do not lose heart (Galatians 6:9).

If any of this is resonating with your spirit, let's stop right here and say a prayer…

Father, I know there are things in my past that have been holding me down and holding me back, things I've not ever really made right with You. I confess it all to You, Lord. I repent of letting it become a stronghold in my life and I ask Your forgiveness. Lord, I believe You hear me when I pray, so I bring my present problem to You—my mountain of need—and by faith, I put it in Your capable hands. I surrender it to You and I release my faith, believing that You will remove it. In Jesus' name, I pray. Amen.

Faith that moves mountains is the God-kind of faith. And He has placed that kind of faith inside of you.

Now, rejoice…call it done…and begin to expect the miracle you've been waiting on!

MY HEALING CONFESSIONS…

- *As I use my faith and plant my seeds of faith, speaking to my mountain (my problem, my sickness), I am setting my faith and believing it will be removed from me.* (James 2:26)

- *When I pray, I will not doubt in my heart but will believe that what I SAY, in faith, will come to pass.* (Mark 11:23-24)

CHAPTER 5

God Is on Your Side

When Jesus walked this earth some 2,000 years ago, He was constantly healing people. He was either on His way to heal somebody or He was in the NOW of their lives, healing them.

That's why I can say, "Jesus is a Healing Jesus."

That's why I can say also… No matter what kind of problem you may be facing, whether it's physical sickness, finances, trouble in your family, pain or confusion in your emotions, estrangement or separation in a marital relationship or in your relationship with God, Jesus wants you to be healed and whole in every area of your life.

How can you effectively serve Him if you are constantly sick and tired? How can you love Him with all your heart, soul and might (Deuteronomy 6:5 KJV) if you are depressed, fearful or anxious?

God is on your side. His greatest desire is that you be in health and prospering (3 John 2). He loves you with a love that never ends, and nothing in this world can ever separate you from His love (Romans 8:35). And, He has promised in His Word that He will never leave you or forsake you (Hebrews 13:5).

In fact, God's love for you is so great that He gave His Son, Jesus, to die on a cruel Cross so that you might be reconciled to God, know Him in a personal relationship, live an abundant life in Jesus and then go to live with Him forever when your time on earth is done (Isaiah 53:5 & John 3:16-17).

In Exodus 15:26, God said, *"I am the Lord who heals you."* Notice, God said, I AM, not I used to be or I will be someday. He said I AM! That's because God never changes (Hebrews 13:8). What we saw Him do in Bible days, He is still doing, today! It's His nature to save, heal and deliver.

You may say, Well, if it's God's nature to heal me, then why am I still sick?

I'll tell you why... It's because there is a devil in this world. And he comes for only three reasons: to steal, to kill and to destroy. But... Jesus came that you might have life and have it more abundantly (John 10:10).

And, another important point to know here is that God will never do anything to violate your free will which He has given you. This may very well be why Jesus often asked people the question, "Will you be made whole?" Or in other words, do you want to be well?

However, you can become a participant in God's healing process by repenting of anything in your life that is contrary to the nature of God—which is in you by the Holy Spirit. Then release your faith and begin expecting the good things from God that He wants you to have.

Don't rehearse and re-hash everything that's wrong. Begin to *call those things which be not as though they were* (Romans 4:17). No, it isn't wishful thinking. It's faith. As you delight yourself in the Lord, your faith mixed with His power can cause miraculous things to come into being in your life. *He will grant you the desires and petitions of your heart* (Psalm 37:4 AMP).

MY HEALING CONFESSIONS...

- *As I begin to believe and to speak positive, faith-building scriptures over my life, I am expecting God to change my thoughts and attitudes.* (Philippians 3:15)

- *As I seek God's kingdom first in my life, I believe all that I need will be given to me.* (Matthew 6:33)

CHAPTER 6

Wilt Thou Be Made Whole?

In the city of Jerusalem, there was a public pool called the Pool of Bethesda. Those persons who were blind, crippled or impotent in some way were put there every day beside the pool to beg for alms or to be put into the pool when "an angel stirred the waters." Most of these people were probably poor or destitute. It was just a place of sickness and disease. And it was into this scene that Jesus, the Master, walked.

The Bible says in John chapter 5 that Jesus saw a man who had been brought there daily for 38 years…a man who had not walked for 38 years. Jesus picked out a hard case and there's a reason why…to illustrate that nothing is too hard for Him. No matter how long you've been dealing with something or how bad you think the situation is, Jesus is willing and able to make it right.

Jesus approached this man and asked him, "Wilt thou be made whole?" In other words, "Sir, do you want to be made well?"

It seems an odd question of someone who is crippled and that the man's answer would be obvious. However, he began to make excuses… "I have no man to put me in the pool and I can't get there in time. Another always gets there before me." You see, there was a belief that an angel would come once a year, and stir the waters. Whoever could get into the water first would be healed.

This is the picture of many today. This is one of our many excuses for not being healed… we don't have a man, a helper. Oh, we may have religion. We may have some belief, but we don't have a man. Or, we may go to the other extreme and depend too much on others, on the government, on the economy. What we need is "The Man"—Jesus Christ.

Now, think about it… 38 years of daily sitting by a pool waiting for something to happen is a very long time. I mean, it would seem after all this time, the lame man could have found someone to shove him over to the edge and then just push him in!

But, just like this man, we have to stop laying blame and stop making excuses if we truly want to be made whole. We have to rise up in our faith and believe.

Jesus looked at the man as he lay on the ground and said three things to him.

First of all, Jesus said to him, "Rise." Now, Jesus knew the man could not physically rise up yet. He was speaking to his inner self or spirit-man. He knew the man would never rise up on the outside without first rising up on the inside, for he had been physically and spiritually laying down for 38 years. Jesus was speaking to his mentality, his attitude, his will and determination to believe for his healing.

It is like the story of the little boy who was in school and would not sit down. The teacher told him to sit down over and over, but the boy would not obey. Finally, the teacher took him to a corner of the room and put her hand on the top of his head and sat him down and told him to sit there. The little boy said to her, "Teacher, I may be sitting down on the outside but I'm standing up on the inside!"

We may read this and laugh because it is somewhat humorous. However, willful rebellion in our heart is not something God takes lightly. First Samuel 15:23 says, *For rebellion is as the sin of witchcraft, and stubbornness is as iniquity and idolatry.*

Now, I'm not implying that the man at the Pool of Bethesda was into witchcraft, but it's very possible that after 38 years, he had become stubborn and a bit rebellious and angry at his circumstances.

The second thing Jesus said to him was, "Take up your bed." He had relied on his bed to hold him and carry him. Jesus was saying, *"Now, you pick up your bed and you carry it."*

If you've been seeking a miracle for a long time, I believe Jesus would say to you, today, "Reevaluate your thinking. Stand up to that opposition, that obstacle that's been in your way. Stand up for what you believe. Make the decision to pick up that thing that has attacked or afflicted you, and throw it aside. Determine and declare, by faith, that you'll not let it hinder you any longer!"

Thirdly, Jesus said to the man, "Walk." In other words, reenter the stream of humanity. Get in step, so to speak, with God's Word. You see, no one had likely spoken to this man in this way before. Most likely, he was considered an outcast because of his affliction and may well have been shunned.

But, when Jesus spoke to him with authority, he suddenly began to feel the power of God as it entered his body. And then, after 38 long years, the man was able to leap to his feet—healed by the miraculous power of God.

Friend, it doesn't matter if you've been waiting a week, a month or for many years as this man did. What does matter is whether YOU are ready to rise up in your faith, stop making any more excuses and believe that Jesus wants to and *is willing* to heal. He's just waiting for you to say, "Yes, I want to be made whole."

MY HEALING CONFESSIONS...

- *No more excuses! I will rise up in my faith, stand on God's Word, believing and looking to Him for my healing.* (Ephesians 6:13)

- *I will no longer let my circumstances dictate and override my desire for a healthy and prosperous life so I can serve the Lord with gladness.* (Philippians 3:12-14)

CHAPTER 7

Seven Rules of Faith to Change Your Life

Seven in the Bible represents God's perfect number. It represents wholeness or completeness.

We have unlimited power available to us right now, today, if we will but operate according to God's laws and God's Word. Long before Benjamin Franklin ever discovered the power of electricity, that power was already there. It existed. It was just waiting for man to discover, to harness, to control. And God's power is available and waiting to be recognized and believed in.

Every person is looking for something—spiritually, physically, financially, in our families or in our emotions. And everyone can tap in and touch God's power. Every man, woman, young person or child.

Let me tell you about Naaman from 2 Kings, chapter 5. Naaman was a general of the Syrian army. He was commander in chief of all the expeditionary forces of Syria. He was mighty in battle and had won many military victories. And he was looked upon by the people as a hero because of his many military successes. It was shocking news when Naaman's personal physician discovered that the general had contracted leprosy, for you see, leprosy was an incurable and debilitating disease at that time. Lepers suffered horribly, both physically and emotionally because of how they were shunned and ostracized. Most were sent to live in a leper's colony, away from the rest of society.

And, it was often thought in those days that if you did contract leprosy, it was because you had sinned in some way and that it was a form of punishment.

This brings me to the first rule of faith that I want you to understand…

Rule 1: Recognize sickness and disease as an oppression of the devil.

Jesus was anointed with the Holy Ghost and with power, who went about doing good, healing all who were oppressed of the devil (Acts 10:38).

We must recognize where sickness and disease come from. They are not from God. The scripture above doesn't say Jesus went about doing bad…that's the devil's business. Jesus went about doing good.

You know, you see some people, who when sickness comes, it's like they open wide the door and say, "Well, hello sickness, how are you? I've been expecting you. How long are you going to stay this time? I've got my bed all ready. I've got the thermometer out. I'm ready for you. Let's snuggle up and get cozy while you're here."

Sickness is not your friend! Sickness is death reaching out its icy hand to take you out of existence. **Sickness is an oppression of the devil.**

Now, on one of Naaman's military campaigns in Israel, he took captive a young girl and he assigned her as a helper to his wife. One day she came in to Naaman's wife and said, "Oh, I wish that Naaman were with the prophet Elisha, who is in Samaria, for he would heal him of his leprosy." Thank God for that young woman who knew about the power of God. Naaman heard about what she had said and was grateful for the report and made his plans for his journey to consult with the prophet. Now, here's the second rule of faith…

Rule 2: Believe the message.

In Mark 9:38-39, one of Jesus' disciples was upset because they had found that some other people were casting out demons in the name of Jesus. He said to Jesus, "Lord, there was another group of people who were casting out demons in your name but we told them to quit because they were not one of us." And Jesus said, "Don't tell them to quit, for they can't do anything in my name and speak lightly of me. And if they're not against us, then they're for me."

My friend, the message of God is more important than the messenger. The words of Richard Roberts are not very important, but the Word of God is very important. And you cannot afford to miss out on what God has to say to you. These words for you are not from my brain. God gave me these thoughts to share with you.

The person we get the message from does not have to have any particular label on them…no particular denomination or particular church or special ministry. What did it matter to Naaman that the message came from someone who was a nobody in the eyes of the world? She was in the right place at the right time, and Naaman believed her and believed her message. Jesus said if you can't believe the messenger, believe for the work's sake (John 14:11).

Naaman knew where the prophet Elisha was. So he got all of his horses and chariots and his aides and took gold and silver and changes of clothing and got ready to go. And this leads me to rule number three…

Rule 3: Go where the power is.

Elisha, who lived in Samaria, was God's prophet. And Israel represented God. However, Syria was a nation that worshipped idols. There was much sin and many problems among the Syrians at that time, and somehow Naaman knew he had to get away from all that. It's amazing how sickness and disease can turn a person to thinking about God. In fact, some people never think about God until they get sick. I believe Naaman knew in his spirit that he would have to come back to God. And he wasn't going to do it there in Syria because of all the sin in the country. He recognized he had to go where the power was.

Isn't that like today? It seems as if everyone is involved with everything but God. We need a holy turnaround of people in this nation and around the world who will come back to God.

You may feel as if you're in a place where there's no power in your life. If you're in a church that seems to have no power, perhaps you should find a new church. Go where the man or woman of God is filled with God's Spirit and with His anointing, who preaches the full gospel and where souls are being won to Christ. Go where the prayer of faith is being prayed for the sick and where they are believing in all of God's power to save, heal and deliver.

You know, doctors are against sickness and for health. But there are some ministers who haven't quite made up their minds whether or not it's God's will for people to be well.

Right in the middle of a church service, a woman had a heart attack. A doctor in the house quickly jumped up and began performing CPR on her. I was told that this doctor was doing everything he could to save this woman while the minister stood at the pulpit with his arms folded and just watched.

My God still does miracles! Oh, if you're not in a place where the power of God is demonstrated in signs and wonders (Hebrews 2:4), you may want to find a new place where it is.

Now, as Naaman prepared for his journey, he made a serious mistake. He didn't go to the prophet; he prepared a letter and went to the king of Israel. And when the king read it, he tore his clothing and got angry, saying, "Who do you think I am anyway? Do you think I'm God? Do you think I can perform this miracle? Are you trying to start some kind of war again between Syria and my country?" About that time, a messenger came from the king's court, a messenger from the prophet Elisha. And Elisha said, "Tell Naaman to come to me. Tell him to come to me so that everyone will know there is still a prophet in Israel."

Rule 4: Put your faith in God, not man.

Naaman had acted on the girl's advice, but he went to the wrong place. Yes, you can have confidence in God's ministers, in His prophets and His evangelists and teachers. Have confidence in men and women of God. But, put your faith in God. Don't put your faith in people. Sometimes, people will let you down.

I once heard about a postal employee who was sorting mail and noticed an envelope made out to God. It seemed to be in a child's handwriting and not knowing quite what to do with it, he opened it. A little boy had written and said, "Dear God, you probably know that not too long ago my daddy died and that my mom is having a hard time raising my sister and me. Would you please send us 500 dollars?"

Well, the postal employee was deeply touched and gathered

up all the money he could from all the other employees and he soon had 300 dollars. The little boy had given the address at the bottom of the letter, so he knew where to send it. He put it in the mail and proudly sent it to the little boy. A few weeks later, as he was again sorting mail, there was another letter to God. He couldn't resist and he opened it. It said, "Dear God, thank you for sending the 300 dollars but the next time you send it, would you send it directly to the house because the post office takes out 200 dollars." Put your faith in God, not man.

Naaman took all his chariots and his aides and he went off to find Elisha. Now, Elisha had been forewarned by God that Naaman was coming and that He needed to see a change of attitude in Naaman. You see, Naaman was quite an arrogant and proud man, and Elisha knew that the man's healing hung in the balance and there would need to be some kind of change in his countenance, his personality or in his attitude or he would go back to Syria and die a leper.

However, when Naaman came to Elisha's door, Elisha didn't come out. He sent his aide out instead. The aide said to him, "General Naaman, the prophet told me to tell you to go down and dip seven times in the Jordan River." Naaman got so angry that he just turned around and rode off.

Oftentimes, that's the way it goes with the proud of heart. It's hard to get our will involved. We know God is telling us to do something and we just aren't willing to humble ourselves and do what He says.

I face that all the time. Many people will come to me before a service and want me to pray for them and speak the word of faith over them before they ever hear the preaching of God's Word. I always say no, not because I think they need to hear me, but they need to hear the Word of God. The Bible says, *Faith comes by hearing, and hearing by the Word of the Lord*

(Romans 10:17). Sometimes, you've just got to change your thinking and your attitude.

As Naaman was going off in a huff, offended that the man of God sent out an aide to him instead of coming out himself, one of Naaman's soldiers must have had a thought about it and rode up beside him and said, (I'm paraphrasing here), "Excuse me, General. Sir, you were expecting Elisha to come out and do some great thing. And when he said what he did, you were upset because you knew that the Jordan River is muddy and dirty. You were probably thinking, 'If I'd wanted a bath, I could have taken one at home in Syria's clean waters.' But Sir, I've served under your command and I love and care for you. Your men are loyal to you and we believe in you. We don't want you to die. Sir, wouldn't it be better to humble yourself and do what the prophet said to do?" This leads me to the fifth rule of faith…

Rule 5 - Accept the correction of God.

After hearing what his soldier had to say, Naaman must have thought, (still paraphrasing)… This Elisha knew all about me and saw right through me. He saw my arrogant attitude and knew I needed to humble myself before God. He realized then that he had made yet another mistake in trying to get his healing from the Lord.

That's one of the great things about God. When you realize you've made a mistake, you can get back up and say, "God, I'm sorry. Please forgive me. Help me not to do that again." You can repent before God. Repenting simply means to change your mind so that God can change your heart. You can then see the consequences of not obeying God and make a turnaround in your attitude.

Naaman did just that and went straight to the shore of the Jordan River. He must have plunged himself into those muddy waters and "gone all under for God." This brings me to rule number six…

Rule 6: Lose yourself.

Imagine the contrast in the General—mighty man of valor, arrogant and angry—just a man, now losing himself as he dips in the muddy River Jordan.

It's the same with us. There are many things in life that we would be better off losing. Thoughts and attitudes that are disobedient to the things of God. And when we do that, we can then link up with the limitless power of Jesus Christ.

Surely a new faith must have risen up inside Naaman as he continued to dip until he had dipped seven times as he was told to do. And my seventh rule is…

Rule 7: Get a point of contact.

Elisha had told Naaman to go and dip in the Jordan River seven times. What is that if not a point of contact? A point of contact is something you do and as you do it, you release your faith. A point of contact sets the time to release your faith, letting everything go to God.

There was no healing in those muddy waters, no healing in plunging himself over and over in that river. No, the healing was from God and in obedience to what God's man had told Naaman to do.

Sometimes, when I pray for people, God will impress upon me to ask them to do some of the craziest things you've ever heard of! And sometimes, I wonder why. But if the Lord is saying it, then I do it! Because it's from the Spirit of God.

Can't you just picture Naaman and how his face, his countenance, must have changed as he continued to dip himself? You see, Naaman's miracle was in his obedience. And I believe that's where your answer lies, too.

Scripture says in 1 Samuel 15:22… *obedience is better than sacrifice*. And the Bible tells us that when Naaman came up after the seventh dip, his skin became as a little child's. He was totally healed of leprosy. He went back to Syria, a new man in his spirit and with a relationship with God that he'd never had before. No doubt, Naaman witnessed of his miracle and led many of his people to God.

This is a picture of the power of grace when we humble ourselves before Almighty God.

There is unlimited power in God for you, too! When you get in harmony with God's laws and His rules of faith, nothing shall be impossible!

Friend, if you've had a relationship with God and it's grown cold, maybe this is the time to "repent"…to turn around in your thinking and in your attitude so you can again be in a position to receive all God has for you. Now hear me on this… We've all sinned and fallen short of the glory of God. But even though you may have sinned, a "sinner" is someone who has made sin their way of life. You can rededicate your life to Christ and begin again. Don't let the devil convince you that you've strayed too far or done something God won't forgive. It's not true! The devil is a liar and the father of lies.

If you would like to make that turnaround right now, or if you've never before given your heart and soul to Jesus Christ as your personal Savior, I'd like to pray for you…

In the mighty name of Jesus Christ, I command any and all strongholds from the devil to be loosed and gone from you…any negative or wrong thinking, any attitudes or habits that are not pleasing to God as you humble yourself before Him. I pray for you to be renewed in your spirit and to have a new way of thinking and talking and a new attitude of obedience toward God's Word. Thank You, Lord, for being Savior, Healer, Deliverer and Friend, and I pray that every need will be met in this person's life by Your mighty power. In Jesus' name, amen.

And if you've never asked Jesus into your heart, say this out loud, *"I believe that Jesus is God's Son and that He died for my sin. I confess my sin and I repent and I turn around, because You said in Your Word that if I confess my sin, You are faithful and just to forgive me and to cleanse me from all that is not right before God. From this day forward, I will live for You. Old things have passed away and all things are becoming new in me. In Jesus' name I pray, amen."*

I pray you'll be encouraged and strengthened in your walk with God as you practice the seven rules of faith above. I believe they'll work for you just as they worked for Naaman.

MY HEALING CONFESSIONS...

- *As I humble myself before God, I believe He will exalt me in due time.* (1 Peter 5:6)

- *As I believe for my healing, I will walk out my faith in harmony with other Christians and with God.* (1 Corinthians 12:18-21,25)

CHAPTER 8

A Holy Determination

Now it happened on a certain day, as He was teaching, that there were Pharisees and teachers of the law sitting by, who had come out of every town of Galilee, Judea, and Jerusalem. And the power of the Lord was present to heal them. Then behold, men brought on a bed a man who was paralyzed, whom they sought to bring in and lay before Him. And when they could not find how they might bring him in, because of the crowd, they went up on the housetop and let him down with his bed through the tiling into the midst before Jesus . When He saw their faith, He said to him, "Man, your sins are forgiven you." And the scribes and the Pharisees began to reason, saying, "Who is this who speaks blasphemies? Who can forgive sins but God alone?" But when Jesus perceived their thoughts, He answered and said to them, "Why are you reasoning in your hearts? Which is easier, to say, 'Your sins are forgiven you,' or to say, 'Rise up and walk'? But that you may know that the Son of Man has power on earth to forgive sins"—He said to the man who was paralyzed, "I say to you, arise, take up your bed, and go to your house." Immediately he rose up before them, took up what he had been lying on, and departed to his own house, glorifying God. And they were all amazed, and they glorified God and were filled with fear, saying, "We have seen strange things today" (Luke 5:17-26)!

Four men…men who had such compassion and such a desire for their friend to be healed. But, the crowd was so large and the house was filled with people. Outside, the house was surrounded with people trying to get close to Jesus. There seemed to be no way the four men could get their friend to Him. But they were determined. They had come there for a purpose.

There was such a fire inside them to see their friend healed that they lifted, climbed and maneuvered their friend up onto the roof of the house where Jesus was preaching, saying, "If we have to raise the roof, we're going to see victory in this man's life." And they began to tear a hole in the roof. That's determination!

Jesus must have looked up to see what was going on. Certainly, the splinters and pieces of tile and pieces of the thatched roof or whatever it was made of began to float down. And then, suddenly, He saw the man being lowered.

Now, we don't see Jesus rushing over to the man to lay hands on him to heal him. We don't even see Him speaking the Word of God for his healing. No, the very next thing we hear is, "And when Jesus saw their faith…"

I've often wondered if we can see faith. Can I look at you and see faith in you? Can you look at me and see faith in me? I don't really know. But what I do know is this…

Jesus can see faith. And the Bible said, "When He saw their faith—not just the faith of the paralyzed man, but the faith of his friends—Jesus said, *"Man, your sins are forgiven you."*

Now why would that be Jesus' first statement to this man who had obviously come for healing in his body? I believe it was because Jesus knew something was wrong in the man's life and He had seen the man's faith not only to be healed but to believe for change. He had a holy determination, and Jesus knew he had a repentant heart. Jesus perceived the faith of the paralytic and He said, "Your sins are forgiven." Jesus dealt with his soul first.

The scribes and pharisees who were there got upset when they heard Jesus say this. Verse 21 says, "Who is this man who speaks blasphemies? Who can forgive sins but God alone?"

Let me tell you right now… If you have faith to believe for your miracle and you have a holy determination inside you to see it happen, you will not escape criticism. Jesus didn't. And neither will you. You'll have your own scribes and pharisees who will scoff, mock and criticize. But don't look to the left or to the right. Don't listen to what they say. Stay focused on God's Word and what His promises are for you, for He is faithful.

Paul said in Philippians 3:12-16 MSG… *You've got to stay focused on the goal. I'm not saying that I have this all together, that I have it made. But I am well on my way, reaching out for Christ, who has so wondrously reached out for me. Friends, don't get me wrong: By no means do I count myself an expert in all of this, but I've got my eye on the goal, where God is beckoning us onward—to Jesus. I'm off and running, and I'm not turning back. So let's keep focused on that goal, those of us who want everything God has for us. If any of you have something else in mind, something less than total commitment, God will clear your blurred vision—you'll see it yet! Now that we're on the right track, let's stay on it.*

And in Hebrews 11-12, we're reminded how the saints of old—Noah, Abraham, Sarah, Isaac, Jacob, Joseph, Moses, Rahab and all the prophets—and our Savior and Lord, Jesus, by acts of faith, believed for the impossible and saw it happen…

"Do you know what this means? All these pioneers who blazed the way, all these veterans cheering us on? It means we'd better get on with it. Strip down, start running—and never quit! No extra spiritual fat, no parasitic sins. Keep your eyes on Jesus, who both began and finished this race we're in. Study how he did it. Because he never lost sight of where he was headed—that exhilarating finish in and with God—he could put up with anything along the way: Cross, shame, whatever. And now he's there, in the place of honor, right alongside God. When you find yourselves flagging in your faith, go over that story again, item by item, that long litany of hostility he plowed through. That will shoot adrenaline into your souls* (Hebrews 12:1-3 MSG)!

The scribes and the pharisees said, "Who is this man who speaks blasphemies?" And the Bible says in verse 22, *Jesus perceived their thoughts and He answering, said unto them, "Why are you reasoning in your hearts? Which is easier, to say, 'Your sins are forgiven you,' or to say, 'Rise up and walk'? But that you may know that the Son of Man has power on earth to forgive sins"—He said to the man who was paralyzed, "I say to you arise, take up your bed, and go to your house." Immediately he rose up before them, took up what he had been lying on, and departed to his own house, glorifying God.*

Let me ask you… Will you respond in faith and demonstrate your own holy determination? Will you act on your faith as this man and his four friends did? Or, will you let the naysayers and the scoffers whittle you down until there is no faith left in you?

If you need a healing touch from Jesus today, don't let anything distract you. Let your own holy determination be known to the devil, believing for what you have a Bible-right to have as a child of God. Let your faith rise up in you as never before and release it to God and believe you receive…until you receive it. Now that's a never-give-up attitude! *"For assuredly, I [Jesus] say to you, whoever says to this mountain, 'Be removed and be cast into the sea,' and does not doubt in his heart, but believes that those things he says will be done, he will have whatever he says. Therefore I say to you, whatever things you ask when you pray, believe that you receive them, and you will have them"* (Mark 11:23-24).

MY HEALING CONFESSIONS...

- *As I seek God's direction for my healing, I will remember that He is my Source and I will stay focused on Him and on His Word.* (Philippians 4:19 & Psalm 119:105)

- *I will welcome and accept help and counsel from godly people who believe in and testify of God's power to heal.* (Psalm 119:24)

CHAPTER 9

A Miracle Settles the Issue

Have you ever seen a miracle or experienced a miracle yourself? Or, are you skeptical, thinking miracles ended in Bible days? Or maybe you don't think yourself worthy of God's attention, let alone a miracle from Him.

Let me begin right here by saying it's not your worthiness that brings healing. It's God's grace, His unmerited favor. He looks at your belief in Him and your faith in His Word.

I've seen thousands of healing miracles throughout my ministry—even mass healings in some of my crusades—and I never cease to be amazed at Jesus' compassion and power. His power to heal and to save is just as mighty today as it was in Bible days.

Let's look at an example from Acts chapter 3, of when the apostles, Peter and John, ministered healing in the name of Jesus after His death, burial and resurrection and His subsequent return to Heaven…

Peter and John went to the Temple one afternoon to take part in the three o'clock prayer service. As they approached the Temple, a man lame from birth was being carried in. Each day he was put beside the Temple gate, the one called the Beautiful Gate, so he could beg from the people going into the Temple (Acts 3:1-2 NLT).

Peter and John certainly knew what they believed. There was no guesswork on their part. Jesus had told Peter to come to Him on a stormy sea, and Peter walked on the water and was saved from drowning. Plus, he had seen Jesus heal his own mother-in-law of a high fever.

John was there for all the healing miracles Jesus performed as He ministered to the people. There was no doubt in his heart that Jesus would heal. In fact, Jesus gave His authority to His disciples to bring healing in His name … *Then He called His twelve disciples together and gave them power and authority over all demons, and to cure diseases. He sent them to preach the kingdom of God and to heal the sick* (Luke 9:1-2). So, as they approached this lame man at the Gate Beautiful, they knew the anointing of God was upon them.

When he saw Peter and John about to enter, he asked them for some money. Peter and John looked at him intently, and Peter said, "Look at us!" The lame man looked at them eagerly, expecting some money. But Peter said, "I don't have any silver or gold for you. But I'll give you what I have. In the name of Jesus Christ, the Nazarene, get up and walk!"

In reading this passage of scripture, it does not indicate that the lame man was in anticipation of, or expecting he might be healed that day. He possibly did not believe that God took any notice of him, a lowly beggar. He most likely thought it would be just like all the days before as he lay there, unable to walk and having to beg and rely on other's generosity just to get by. I don't think that he had any idea that the faith of Peter and

John would make this day different from all others and that at the end of it, he would be completely free and able to leap up and walk! He probably couldn't even conceive of the fact that the glory of God was about to shine down upon him!

God often surprises us with His favor. And if you need His healing touch, I encourage you to surround yourself with His presence. You don't have to go to a special place or even be in a church service to receive from God.

We must come to the point where it's easy to get healed… and you do that by feeding on God and His Word. We must feed our spirits on the life of Jesus—on His ways of doing and being—and not on the world's ways. Jesus stretches out His arms and beckons us… *Come unto me, all ye that labour and are heavy laden, and I will give you rest. Take my yoke upon you, and learn of me; for I am meek and lowly in heart: and ye shall find rest unto your souls* (Matthew 11:28-29 KJV).

Right where you are, you can begin to *enter His gates with thanksgiving and into His courts with praise* (Psalm 100:4). Thank Him, worship Him and put yourself into an atmosphere for healing, for *God inhabits the praises of His people* (Psalm 22:3).

Then Peter took the lame man by the right hand and helped him up. And as he did, the man's feet and ankles were instantly healed and strengthened. He jumped up, stood on his feet, and began to walk! Then, walking, leaping, and praising God, he went into the Temple with them.

All the people saw him walking and heard him praising God. When they realized he was the lame beggar they had seen so often at the Beautiful Gate, they were absolutely astounded! They all rushed out in amazement to Solomon's Colonnade, where the man was holding tightly to Peter and John.

The religious leaders of the day thought they had put an end to this Jesus, but now, His disciples were doing what He had done. They said, *"What shall we do to these men? For, indeed, that a notable miracle has been done through them is evident to all who dwell in Jerusalem, and we cannot deny it"* (Acts 4:16).

I tell you, a miracle settles the issue! It can't be denied when you see it with your own eyes. It shuts the mouth of the enemy. It's the undeniable manifestation of the power and glory of God. The evidence of it is there for all to see.

Peter saw his opportunity and addressed the crowd. "People of Israel," he said, "what is so surprising about this? And why stare at us as though we had made this man walk by our own power or godliness? For it is the God of Abraham, Isaac, and Jacob—the God of all our ancestors—who has brought glory to his servant Jesus by doing this. Through faith in the name of Jesus, this man was healed—and you know how crippled he was before. Faith in Jesus' name has healed him before your very eyes."

I firmly believe that we are again coming into a time of "notable miracles." A time like no other; a time of revival and of great trust and faith in the Lord God. A new level of miracles that we've never experienced before…amazing "signs and wonders" that will be a witness to the unbelieving world that Jesus is who He says He is.

Be expecting it. But more than that, be expecting your miracle of healing. Whatever your greatest need is, Jesus is in the NOW of your life. He's not the "I was." He's the great *I AM!* Pray, believe and expect.

MY HEALING CONFESSIONS...

- *As I meditate on God's Word and pray, believing, I will be expecting God's miracle touch in my life.* (Philippians 1:6)

- *I will not give in to discouragement or depression but will continually hope in the Lord.* (Psalm 43:5)

CHAPTER 10

I Hate Cancer!

Jesus healed all manner of sickness and disease. —Matthew 4:23

I absolutely hate cancer! I hate it with all my being. I hate what it does to the individual suffering from its effects and I hate what it does to that person's family, who not only go through the trauma with the sick person, but who often have to endure financial hardship for years to come because of the cost of treatment.

Satan, our enemy, loves this disease. It's diabolical and he's used it to take out millions of people. In fact, 1.6 million Americans receive this diagnosis in an average year.

The "C word" strikes fear and terror in the hearts of many. I certainly can empathize and understand. My own dear wife, Lindsay, was diagnosed with thyroid cancer a few years ago. Praise God, He helped us prepare for Lindsay's healing. He gave us direction and guidance as we made the necessary decisions regarding her treatment. We put all our fear, worry and concern on the Lord. Lindsay's doctors recommended surgery and today, she is cancer-free!

Friend, Jesus is a Healing Jesus! And cancer is no harder for Him to heal than a toothache or a headache. *Nothing is impossible with God* (Luke 1:37)!

Cancer is a disease. That's dis-ease; it's a discomfort that is not supposed to be in your body. It is contrary to the healing Jesus provided for on the Cross of Calvary… *But He was wounded for our transgressions, He was bruised for our iniquities; the chastisement for our peace was upon Him, and by His stripes we are healed* (Isaiah 53:5).

Notice the last line in the verse above…***we are healed***. Not, one day you'll be healed or possibly, if it's the Lord's will, you'll be healed. No! It says you are already healed, by faith in Jesus and His finished work on the Cross.

I want to give you some steps you can take which I believe can put you into position to receive your healing…wholeness and healing in any area…but particularly, if you or a loved one has received a diagnosis of cancer.

Step 1: Understand that Jesus has already paid the price for your healing.

It's a done deal! When you go into a store and make a cash purchase, that item is now yours. You paid the cost and it belongs to you. Jesus paid the ultimate price for us by willingly sacrificing His life on the Cross. Salvation, provision and healing belong to you. When you received Jesus into your heart as your Lord and Savior, these things He purchased for you become your inheritance as God's child.

Step 2: Begin digging into the Word of God.

You have a Bible-right to all God has for you…and you

receive it by faith. Faith is simply believing what God says in His Word. It's trusting what He says more than what the diagnosis says. So, how does faith come? *Faith comes by hearing and hearing by the word of God* (Romans 10:17). If you want your faith to mature so you can believe for healing from cancer, then start digging into the Word of God as never before. Begin to believe as you read the promises of God. Think on them, meditate on them and pray them over yourself often.

Step 3: Learn from trusted men and women of God.

Take the time to seek out persons who have a proven record of having God's anointing on their lives and ministries for healing. You don't necessarily have to go to them in person to have them lay hands on you. Many of them have websites and a presence on social media where you can follow their teaching and receive their prayers. They themselves have often experienced supernatural healing, and they understand what you're going through. They will teach you biblical principles to stand on and to stand against your symptoms and help you believe for your complete healing.

Step 4: Begin to speak out God's truths concerning healing.

Build yourself up on your most holy faith. (Jude 1:20) Begin to speak out the scriptures regarding healing. Make them personal. Say them over and over again until you get them deep down into your spirit.

Scriptures like:

- 1 Peter 2:24 — *By Jesus' stripes, I am healed.*
- Matthew 4:23 — *Jesus is healing all manner of sickness and disease in me.*

- Matthew 14:14 — *Jesus is moved with compassion for me and He is healing this sickness in me.*

- Exodus 15:26 — *God is the Lord my healer.*

- Psalm 103:3 — *God forgives all my sin and heals all my diseases.*

- Psalm 107:20 — *God sent His Word and healed me and delivered me from my destruction.*

- Psalm 118:17 — *I shall live and not die and I will declare the works of the Lord.*

- Nahum 1:9 — *This affliction shall be gone from me and not rise up a second time.*

- James 5:16 — *I am confessing my faults and praying for others that I may be healed.*

(This is a short list of healing scriptures. As you confess them, apply them to your life. For other resources such as CDs, DVDs and books on healing, visit our website at **RichardRoberts.org**.)

Even if you're still dealing with symptoms and pain and side effects, proclaim that you are healed. Continue to proclaim it and expect the symptoms to begin to subside.

Step 5: Practice good health habits and take care of your body.

God has given you an amazing gift, a human body. Within it, He designed systems to help you to heal. Take advantage of the many resources available to you which are good for your overall health. God works through doctors and specialists, so defer to your physician's plan for your recovery and suggestions for optimum health.

Step 6: Make use of your communication system with God, the Holy Spirit.

The Holy Spirit is the center of the communication between you and God, and only He can give you clear direction because He knows the heart of the Father. Pray in the spirit and then pray with your own understanding. God may give you insights about helpful things to do that you may not have thought of.

Step 7: Get rid of any unforgiveness in your heart.

If you're holding on to something or have a grudge against someone, let it go. Forgive them. I didn't say forget…I said forgive. Unforgiveness can hold you back in unimaginable ways and can actually hinder your physical healing. Don't let unforgiveness be an obstacle that stands in the way of your complete recovery.

These are some of the steps Lindsay and I took together as we stood in faith for her healing, and I believe they will be a help to you also. God loves you; He's your Heavenly Father. And just as a loving father here on earth would do anything to see his own child healthy and happy, you can expect God to move heaven and earth to get His healing power to you, too.

MY HEALING CONFESSIONS...

- *As I confess the scriptures from this chapter, I believe that ALL God's promises for me are true. He loves me and He wants me well.*

- *Cancer comes from the enemy of my soul and I declare it does not have the authority to be in my body. I am God's property and nothing is too hard for my God!* (Jeremiah 32:17)

CHAPTER 11

You Are a Part of Your Answer

Believe it or not, people will often ask me if I truly believe it is God's will to heal. It's kind of incredulous to me…after all, I am an evangelist in the healing ministry and it's my calling to operate in God's anointing that is on me to pray and believe for healing miracles. Of course, I believe He still heals!

And, over the years, I've had a lot of people ask me, "If God heals, why doesn't He just make me well?"

Yes, it's true that God is a sovereign God. He can act arbitrarily and sometimes does.

But, in my experience, the availability of His healing power is only one part of the equation for your healing. The other part of the healing process is you.

If you study the life and ministry of Jesus in the Gospels, we see Him, time and again, healing people and bringing deliverance into their lives. So, clearly, it's God's will to heal all those who come to Him.

But, one thing you need to understand about healing is this… Just because healing is God's will does not mean it always comes to us automatically.

Sometimes we humans get so used to talking about the situation, the sickness, the problem, that we literally get in the way of our own healing.

It's like the woman who said, "You think you're sick? Let me tell you about my sickness!"

And I believe that sometimes, we give too much credit to the devil by talking so much about the problem and not enough about the answer. Now, I'm not talking about denying the problem or sickness or acting like it's not there. Yes, the problem exists. However, your focus should not be on the problem or sickness itself. Your focus should be upon God who is the Healer.

In Matthew 9:27-30 we read… *"… two blind men followed Him [Jesus], crying out and saying, "Son of David, have mercy on us!" And when He had come into the house, the blind men came to Him. And Jesus said to them, "Do you believe that I am able to do this?" They said to Him, "Yes, Lord." Then He touched their eyes, saying, "According to your faith let it be to you." And their eyes were opened.*

In essence, Jesus was asking the men to use their faith to receive their healing.

Hebrews 11:1 says that *faith is the substance of things hoped for, the evidence of things not seen.*

Everyone has faith. Romans 12:3 tells us that God has given to every person the measure of faith. Not "a measure," but

THE measure. We've all been given the same amount of faith. The question is, are we using it?

Why is your faith so important? Because it has substance, which is an essential ingredient in order to receive your miracle from God. And His Word tells us that it's impossible to please Him without using our faith... *But without faith it is impossible to please Him, for he who comes to God must believe that He is, and that He is a rewarder of those who diligently seek Him* (Hebrews 11:6).

There was no question as to God's perfect will in healing those two blind men. But in order for them to experience it, they had to take the responsibility for the manifestation of that miracle by exercising their faith.

Consider this statement... *Without God, I cannot. But without me, He will not.*

You see, there is to be a divine reciprocity between God and you...a divine connection of agreement.

Jesus said in Matthew 18:18-19... *"Assuredly, I say to you, whatever you bind on earth will be bound in heaven, and whatever you loose on earth will be loosed in heaven. Again I say to you that if two of you agree on earth concerning anything that they ask, it will be done for them by My Father in heaven."*

Think about it... In what we refer to as the Lord's Prayer in Matthew 6, Jesus taught His disciples, and us, to pray, *"Your will be done on earth as it is in Heaven."*

So, what is Heaven like? No death, no pain, no sorrow, no sickness or disease, no darkness or separation, no lack of any kind.

There has to be an agreement between you and God, and you must speak His language, not yours. You have to come into agreement with His Word.

You can't pray and say you believe God is healing you and then turn around and say something like, "Well, I hope that worked." You must hold on to the promise, continuing to speak God's Word over yourself and your situation, believing for your miracle to manifest. That's the faith-walk.

I'd like to invite you to come into agreement with me and with God's Word right now for your healing. Let's pray…

In the mighty name of Jesus, Name that is above all other names in Heaven and on earth, I speak healing and wholeness to you. I rebuke Satan and I command him to take his hands off of you for he has no authority or business in the life of a child of God. I speak to every symptom of illness that is in your body and I tell them to GO, in Jesus' name! And I speak healing…from the top of your head to the soles of your feet. May you be healed, by the mighty healing power of Jesus which fows through you. In His Name I pray, amen.

Friend, come into agreement with God's Word and be a part of your miracle answer. And not only for healing in your physical body, but if you are suffering lack in your finances, I encourage you to come into agreement with God's Word in the area of tithing and giving and begin to practice His principles concerning seed-time and harvest.

If you want to see the extraordinary in your life, then you must be responsible for exercising your faith. Don't just wish and hope it happens. Be a participant in the process…and expect God to meet you where you are.

MY HEALING CONFESSIONS…

- *I am exercising my faith in God's Word and in His ability and willingness to heal me. I am seeking His direction and guidance for living a healthy and prosperous life.* (James 1:5)

- *I will speak out and think only on those things that contribute to my spiritual and physical well-being.* (Philippians 4:8)

CHAPTER 12

Fueled by Faith

If I can but touch his clothes, I will be healed. —Matthew 9:21

That's what she told herself, this nameless, suffering woman, fueled by nothing but her faith.

It was a daring plan. According to Mosaic Law, women who were ceremonially unclean weren't even allowed to touch anyone. But she was desperate, and desperate people do desperate things.

The story is told in Mark 5... *Now a certain woman had a flow of blood for twelve years, and had suffered many things from many physicians. She had spent all that she had and was no better, but rather grew worse. When she heard about Jesus, she came behind Him in the crowd and touched His garment. For she said, "If only I may touch His clothes, I shall be made well."*

Immediately the fountain of her blood was dried up, and she felt in her body that she was healed of the affliction. And Jesus, immediately knowing in Himself that power had gone out of Him, turned around in the crowd and said, "Who touched My clothes?" But His disciples said to Him, "You see the multitude thronging You, and You say, 'Who touched Me?'"

And He looked around to see her who had done this thing. But the woman, fearing and trembling, knowing what had happened to her, came and fell down before Him and told Him the whole truth. And He said to her, "Daughter, your faith has made you well. Go in peace, and be healed of your affliction."

Can you just imagine her fear and trepidation as she tried to get close to Jesus? She must have heard from others that this was someone who performed miracles, and after twelve long years of being physically sick and socially outcast because of a continuous blood flow from her body, she was willing to risk everything.

She was probably so very tired and may have been weak. But more than just being physically exhausted because of her illness, she must have also been weary in heart and spirit. She had spent all she had on physicians trying to relieve her suffering, but she only grew worse.

Somehow, the woman was able to make her way through the crowd and quietly touched the hem of Jesus' garment. By law, her touch would have made Him unclean. But… by grace, just the opposite happened. Immediately her bleeding stopped, and she knew she would never be the same from that day forward.

We're told in Hebrews 11:6 that *without faith it is impossible to please him: for he that cometh to God must believe that he is, and that he is a rewarder of them that diligently seek him.*

You may know exactly how this woman felt. Run down, ostracized, lonely, laughed at and mocked, embarrassed and frustrated, she made use of the one thing that had remained healthy: her faith.

And there is no difference today. God is no respecter of persons (Acts 10:34). You, as a believer in Jesus, can reach out to Him with your faith and believe for His miracle touch.

It doesn't matter if you've been afflicted for some time like this woman in the Bible or if you've just recently received a negative diagnosis. Pray, release your faith and believe. Speak His Word over yourself, even if you're still experiencing symptoms of the illness.

God loves you and He wants to make you well. You can be cleansed; you can be healed. Dare to be bold and to be fueled by *your* faith.

MY HEALING CONFESSIONS...

- *I am bold in my faith for healing because God is faithful.* (Hebrews 10:23)

- *I will give thanks in everything and sing praises unto my God who is my Helper.* (Philippians 4:6 & Psalm 30:10-12)

CHAPTER 13

Summary

God, our loving heavenly Father, wants to see people made whole and to be free from sickness and disease. And that's why I wrote this book. Because I want people to know this truth.

God knows and understands that we can't live productive lives—or sometimes even carry out His will for our lives—if we are living with constant pain or are otherwise unhealthy in some way.

Here is a short summary of the biblical principles I've outlined for you in *God's Healing Touch*. I pray that you'll read them over and over until they get deep down into your spirit and that you'll see your miracle come to pass as you put them into practice in your own life…

- Know that it's God's will for you to be healed in every area of your life…spirit, soul and body (3 John 2). Believe the promises in His Word.

- Be assured that your healing has already been paid for in full by Jesus.

- Unconfessed and unrepented sin needs to be dealt with.

- Forgiveness has to be a part of your healing process.

- Go into agreement with God's Word for your healing. Pray in the authority you have in the name of Jesus.

- Stop focusing on the problem (the sickness) and talk up the Answer. Confess healing scriptures. Say them out loud and keep on saying them until your miracle comes.

- Release your faith and EXPECT your miracle.

Although I certainly don't claim to have all the answers on the subject of God's healing power, my prayer for you is that through revelation from the Holy Spirit and the illumination of God's Word, and through any insight you may have gathered from reading *God's Healing Touch*, you can now begin to see how much God desires for you to be well, and, how you can move forward into health and prosperity by participating in His healing process.

For prayer, call

The Abundant Life Prayer Group at

918-495-7777,

or contact us online at

www.RichardRoberts.org

RICHARD ROBERTS

Richard Roberts, B.A., M.A., D.Min., is the Chairman and CEO of Richard Roberts Ministries and has dedicated his life to ministering the saving, healing, delivering power of Jesus Christ around the world.

Richard has ministered God's healing power in 39 nations, spanning six continents. In his healing outreaches, Richard has ministered to crowds of over 200,000 people in a single service. His services are marked with supernatural miracles and healings and by a tremendous move of the Spirit. Today, Richard focuses on his *Greater Works* International Pastor's Conferences where he teaches and trains pastors in underdeveloped nations to take the full gospel–with miracles, healing and signs following–to their villages, cities, and nations, as Jesus said in John 14:12.

Richard and his wife, Lindsay, also host *The Place for Miracles*—a half-hour inspirational TV broadcast that reaches out to millions worldwide. Together, Richard and Lindsay minister in the power of the Holy Spirit, praying for those who need a miracle of healing in some area of their lives.

In 2010, Richard founded the *Richard Roberts School of Miracles* which offers online Bible courses to help equip Christians with practical, hands-on experience in applying God's Word and His healing power in their own lives and in the lives of others. These courses emphasize how believers can enjoy a life empowered by the Holy Spirit.

In May 2023 Richard and Lindsay launched a powerful, new resource for healing! **The Healing Network**…it's "all healing, all the time." This 24-hour network is your place for live healing prayer, anointed messages, faith building resources, miracle testimonies and much more!

In addition, Richard hosts a weekly podcast, *Expect a Miracle*, sharing teachings and conversations to inspire listeners to expect the miracles they need in life. He has also authored a number of publications and other inspirational material, including …*Your Road to a Better Life, Unstoppable Increase, He's A Healing Jesus, God's Healing Touch,* and *Thrive—Eliminating Lack from Your Life*.

www.RichardRoberts.org